Ewé Osanyin

180 Herbs Commonly Used in Ifá-Orisha
(Scientific/Spanish/Yoruba Name)
180 Hierbas de uso común en Ifá-Orisha
(Nombre latino/cubano/lucumí)

Baba Jaha

blue ocean press
tokyo

Published by:

blue ocean press,
an Imprint of Aoishima Research Institute (ARI)
#807-36 Lions Plaza Ebisu
3-25-3 Higashi, Shibuya-ku
Tokyo, Japan 150-0011
mail@aoishima-research.org

URL: http://www.blueoceanpublications.com
        http://www.aoishima-research.org

ISBN: 978-4-902837-93-3

Table of Contents

180 Herbs Used in Ifá-Orisha/180 Hierbas de uso común en Ifá-Orisha

Scientific Name (Nombre latino) - Spanish Name (Nombre cubano) - Yoruba Name (Nombre lucumí)   Picture #

180 Herbs Used in Ifá-Orisha
180 Hierbas de uso común en Ifá-Orisha

Scientific Name (Nombre latino)
ABRUS PRECATORIUS

Spanish Name (Nombre cubano)
PEONÍA

Yoruba Name (Nombre lucumí)
EWERENJENJÉ

1

Scientific Name (Nombre latino)
ACHRAS SAPOTE

Spanish Name (Nombre cubano)
ZAPOTE

Scientific Name (Nombre latino)
ACHRAS ZAPOTA

Spanish Name (Nombre cubano)
MAMEY COLORADO

Yoruba Name (Nombre lucumí)
EMÍ

Scientific Name (Nombre latino)
ACROCOMIA CRISPA (ELAEIS GUINEENSIS)

Spanish Name (Nombre cubano)
COROJO

Yoruba Name (Nombre lucumí)
EKPÓ, EPÓ, EPO PUPO, LUFI

Scientific Name (Nombre latino)
ADENOROPIUM GOSSYPIFOLIUM

Spanish Name (Nombre cubano)
FRAILECILLO, CAIRECILLO DE MONTE

Yoruba Name (Nombre lucumí)
BASIGÜÉ, PÁIME

Scientific Name (Nombre latino)
ADIANTUM TENERUM
(ADIANTUM CAPILLUS VENERIS)

Spanish Name (Nombre cubano)
CULANTRILLO DE POZO

Yoruba Name (Nombre lucumí)
KOTONIO, OFI, NECENTÉN

6

Scientific Name (Nombre latino)
AFRAMOMUN MELEGUETA

Spanish Name (Nombre cubano)
PIMIENTA DE GUINEA

Yoruba Name (Nombre lucumí)
ATÁ, ATARE

Scientific Name (Nombre latino)
ALLIUM CEPA

Spanish Name (Nombre cubano)
CEBOLLA

Yoruba Name (Nombre lucumí)
ALÚBOSA, ELLA SRO

Scientific Name (Nombre latino)
ALLIUM SATIVUM

Spanish Name (Nombre cubano)
AJO

Yoruba Name (Nombre lucumí)
JOKOIO EWÉCO, ALU DESO GUERE

9

Scientific Name (Nombre latino) ALLOPHYLLUS COMINIA

Spanish Name (Nombre cubano)
PALO CAJA

Yoruba Name (Nombre lucumí)
IGGI BIRÉ, OÍN, MEREMBE

Scientific Name(Nombre latino)
ALPINIA AROMATICA
(ALPINIA SPECIOSA SCHUM)

Spanish Name (Nombre cubano)
COJATE, COATE, COLONIA

Yoruba Name (Nombre lucumí)
ORÚ, OBURO, DIDONA

Scientific Name (Nombre latino)
AMAIOUA CORYMBOSA

Spanish Name (Nombre cubano)
PALO CAFÉ

Yoruba Name (Nombre lucumi)
IGGIFERE, APÓ

Scientific Name (Nombre latino)
AMARANTHUS CAUDATUS

Yoruba Name (Nombre lucumi)
EWE TELE

Scientific Name (Nombre latino)
AMARANTHUS VIRIDIS

Spanish Name (Nombre cubano)
BLEDO

Yoruba Name (Nombre lucumí)
LOBÉ, EWE TETÉ
(CHAURÉ KUE KUE E WEIKO)

Scientific Name (Nombre latino)
AMBROSIA ARTEMISIFOLIA
(COCHLEARIA CORONOPUS)

Spanish Name (Nombre cubano)
ALTAMISA, ARTEMISA

Yoruba Name (Nombre lucumí)
LINIDDI

Scientific Name (Nombre latino)
AMYRIS BALSAMIFERA

Spanish Name (Nombre cubano)
GUABA

Yoruba Name (Nombre lucumí)
LOASO

Scientific Name (Nombre latino)
ANANAS ANANAS
(ANANAS COMOSUS)

Spanish Name (Nombre cubano)
PIÑA BLANCA

Yoruba Name (Nombre lucumí)
EGBOIBO, OPPÖYIBO

Scientific Name (Nombre latino)
ANNONA MURICATA

Spanish Name (Nombre cubano)
GUANÁBANA

Yoruba Name (Nombre lucumí)
IGGI OMÓ FUNFÚN, GWÁNILLO, NICHULARAFÚN

Scientific Name (Nombre latino)
ANREDERA SPICATA (HEDERA HELIX)

Spanish Name (Nombre cubano)
YEDRA

Yoruba Name (Nombre lucumí)
ITAKO

Scientific Name (Nombre latino)
ARACHIS HYPOGAEA

Spanish Name (Nombre cubano)
MANÍ

Yoruba Name (Nombre lucumí)
EPÁ, EPAMILBO, EFÁ, EWA, BUSIA

Scientific Name (Nombre latino)
ARGEMONE MEXICANA

Spanish Name (Nombre cubano)
CARDO SANTO

Yoruba Name (Nombre lucumí)
IKA, AGOGÓ, IGBEELEGÚN, EEKANNA EKUN

Scientific Name (Nombre latino)
ARTEMISIA ABROTANUM
(ARTEMISIA CAMPHORATA)

Spanish Name (Nombre cubano)
INCIENSO

Yoruba Name (Nombre lucumí
TURARÉ, MINSELO

Scientific Name (Nombre latino)
BAMBUSA VULGARIS

SPANISH Name (Nombre cubano)
CAÑA BRAVA

Scientific Name (Nombre latino)
BIXA ORELLANA

Spanish Name (Nombre cubano)
BIJA

Yoruba Name (Nombre lucumí)
OEN

24

Scientific Name (Nombre latino)
BOERHAAVIA ERECTA CARIBAEA

Spanish Name (Nombre cubano)
ATIPONLA

YORUBA NAME (Nombre lucumi)
ATIPONLA

Scientific Name/Nombre latino
CAESALPINIA BONDUC

Spanish Name/Nombre cubano
QUITA MALDICIÓN

Yoruba Name/Nombre lucumi
EWE AYO, ABERIKUNLÓ

Scientific Name (Nombre latino)
CALALU

Spanish Name (Nombre cubano)
CALALÚ

Yoruba Name (Nombre lucumí)
CALALÚ

Scientific Name (Nombre latino)
CALYCOPHILLUM CANDIDISSIMUM

Spanish Name (Nombre cubano)
DAGAME

Yoruba Name (Nombre lucumí)
LIONSE

Scientific Name (Nombre latino)
CAMERARIA LATIFOLIA

Spanish Name (Nombre cubano)
MABOA

Yoruba Name (Nombre lucumí)
LÉCHU IBAYÉ

Scientific Name (Nombre latino)
CAPRARIA BIFLORA

Spanish Name (Nombre cubano)
ESCLABIOSA, ESCLAVIOSA

Yoruba Name (Nombre lucumí)
GAÚTI

Scientific Name (Nombre latino)
CAPSICUM BACCATUM

Spanish Name (Nombre cubano)
AJÍ GUAGUAO

Yoruba Name (Nombre lucumi)
ATÁ, GUAGUAO

31

Scientific Name (Nombre latino)
CARICA PAPAYA

Spanish Name (Nombre cubano)
FRUTA BOMBA, PAPAYA

Yoruba Name (Nombre lucumí)
IDEFÉ, IBEKUÉ, IBEPPE

Scientific Name (Nombre latino)
CASEARIA HIRSUTA

Spanish Name (Nombre cubano)
RASPA LENGUA

Yoruba Name (Nombre lucumí)
EWE ELÉNU, YERÉOBO

Scientific Name (Nombre latino)
CASSIA OCCIDENTALIS
(CASSIA TORA)

Spanish Name (Nombre cubano)
GUANINA, HIERBA HEDIONDA

Yoruba Name (Nombre lucumí)
JASISAN KROPOMU, YAASO,
JARA–JARA, AYEGUÉ, OYÉUN, OYEUSÁ, JARA-JARA,
EWE TOMODE

Scientific Name (Nombre latino)
CATHARANTHUS ROSEUS

Spanish Name (Nombre cubano)
VICARIA

Scientific Name (Nombre latino)
GECROPIA PELTATA

Spanish Name (Nombre cubano)
YAGRUMA

Yoruba Name (Nombre lucumí)
IGGI, OGGUGÚ, OGUGUN, OGÚN GUN, OGGÚ, LORO,
LARA, LARO

Scientific Name (Nombre latino)
CEDRELA MEXICANA
(CITRUS MEDICA)

Spanish Name (Nombre cubano)
CEDRO

Yoruba Name (Nombre lucumí)
OPEPÉ, ROKÓ

Scientific Name (Nombre latino)
CEIBA PENTANDRA
(CEIBA CASEARIA)

Spanish Name (Nombre cubano)
CEIBA

Yoruba Name (Nombre lucumí)
ARABBÁ, ALABA, ARÁGGUO,
IROKO, IROKO TERÉ, IROKO–AWO, ELÚWERE, ELUÉCO,
ASABÁ (IGGI ARABBÁ), IGGI OLORUN

Scientific Name (Nombre latino)
CELOSIA ARGENTEA

Spanish Name (Nombre cubano)
CRESTA DE GALLO

Yoruba Name (Nombre lucumí)
LIBBE KUKO

Scientific Name (Nombre latino)
CESTRUM DIURNUM

Spanish Name (Nombre cubano)
GALÁN DE DÍA

Yoruba Name (Nombre lucumí)
ORUFIRIN, TOÍRO

Scientific Name (Nombre latino)
CHENOPODIUM AMBROSIODES

Spanish Name (Nombre cubano)
APASOTE

Yoruba Name (Nombre lucumí)
OLINE

Scientific Name (Nombre latino)
CHRYSOPHILLUM CAINITO

Spanish Name (Nombre cubano)
CAIMITO

Yoruba Name (Nombre lucumí)
ASÁN, ALLECOFOLE, OSÁM, OGÓE FUSÉ, AYÉCO FOLÉ

Scientific Name (Nombre latino)
CINNAMOMUM CASSIA
(CINNAMOMUM ZEYLANICUM)

Spanish Name (Nombre cubano)
CANELA DE MONTE,
CANELA DE CHINA

Yoruba Name (Nombre lucumí)
IGGI EPÓ KAN, DEDÉ, KOROKOLO

Scientific Name (Nombre latino)
CISSAMPELOS MUCRONATA

Spanish Name (Nombre cubano)
DEJAME SENTARME

Scientific Name (Nombre latino)
CISSUS SICYOIDES
(CISSUS QUADRANGULARIS)

Spanish Name (Nombre cubano)
BEJUCO UBÍ, BEJUCO UVÍ

Yoruba Name (Nombre lucumí)
EGGUÉLE KERI

Scientific Name (Nombre latino)
CITRULLUS CITRULLUS
(CITRULLUS LANATUS)

Spanish Name (Nombre cubano)
MELÓN DE AGUA

Yoruba Name (Nombre lucumí)
AGBÉYE, AGUE TUTÚ, ITAKÚN
OYÉ, OGGURE, EGURIN

Scientific Name (Nombre latino)
CITRUS AURANTIUM
(CITRUS SINENSIS)

Spanish Name (Nombre cubano)
NARANJA

Yoruba Name (Nombre lucumí) OROLOCUM, ORÓMBO,
OLÓMBO, OSÁN, QEBURUKÚ, OSAEYÍMBO, ESÁ

Scientific Name (Nombre latino)
CITRUS AURANTIUM, VAR. AMARA
(CITRUS VULGARIS)

Spanish Name (Nombre cubano)
NARANJA AGRIA

Yoruba Name (Nombre lucumí)
KOROSÁN

Scientific Name (Nombre latino)
CITRUS LIMON

Spanish Name (Nombre cubano)
LIMÓN

Yoruba Name (Nombre lucumí)
OROCO, OROMBOUEUE, OLOMBO

Scientific Name (Nombre latino)
COCOS NUCIFERA

Spanish Name (Nombre cubano)
COCO

Yoruba Name (Nombre lucumí)
OBI

Scientific Name (Nombre latino)
COFFEA ARABICA

Spanish Name (Nombre cubano)
CAFÉ

Yoruba Name (Nombre lucumí)
OBIMOTIGWÁ, IGGI KAN, EKÁNCHACHAETÉ,
OMATIWAOSEGÜÍ,
OSINA BONA, OMÍ DUDU

Scientific Name (Nombre latino)
COMMELINA ELEGANS

Spanish Name (Nombre cubano)
CANUTILLO

Yoruba Name (Nombre lucumí)
KARODO, KORODO,
CARRODDO, CARODI COTONÉMBO, COTONEMBO, COTOLO,
IBAKUÁ MINOCUÍ, MINI

Scientific Name (Nombre latino)
CORCHORUS OLITORIUS

Spanish Name (Nombre cubano)
MALVA TÈ, GUENGUERÉ

Yoruba Name (Nombre lucumí)
EFO

Scientific Name (Nombre latino)
CORCHORUS SILIQUOSUS

Yoruba Name (Nombre lucumí)
DEDÉ

Scientific Name (Nombre latino)
CORDIA COLLOCOCCA

Spanish Name (Nombre cubano)
ATEJE COMUN

Yoruba Name (Nombre lucumí)
LACHEO, LÁNGWE

Scientific Name (Nombre latino)
CRESCENTIA CUJETE

Spanish Name (Nombre cubano)
GÜIRA

Yoruba Name (Nombre lucumí)
EGGWÁ, IGBÁ, AGBÉ,
AGGÜÉ, EGWÁ

Scientific Name (Nombre latino)
CUCURBITA MAXIMA

Spanish Name (Nombre cubano)
CALABAZA

Yoruba Name (Nombre lucumí)
ELEGUEDDÉ

Scientific Name (Nombre latino)
CUPANIA CUBENSIS

Spanish Name (Nombre cubano)
GUARA

Yoruba Name (Nombre lucumi)
GUARÁ, AGAGWAN

Scientific Name (Nombre latino)
CURCAS CURCAS
(JATROPHA CURCAS)

Spanish Name (Nombre cubano)
PIÑON BOTIJA

Yoruba Name (Nombre lucumí)
ADDÓ, ALUMOFO, AKUNU, OLOBOTUYA, OLÉ IYÉTEBE

Scientific Name (Nombre latino)
CYNODON DACTYLON
(AGROPYRUM REPENS)

Spanish Name (Nombre cubano)
GRAMA, PATA DE GALLINA

Yoruba Name (Nombre Lucumí)
COTONEMBO, ERAN, DENGO, ELEGGUÉ, TUMAYÁ, IYERAN

Scientific Name (Nombre latino)
DATURA STRAMONIUM

Spanish Name (Nombre cubano)
CHAMICO, TÉ DEL DIABLO

Yoruba Name (Nombre lucumí)
EWE OFÓ, EWE ECHÉNLA

Scientific Name (Nombre latino)
DATURA SUAVEOLENS

Spanish Name (Nombre cubano)
CAMPANA

Yoruba Name (Nombre lucumí)
AGGOGÓ, AGOGÓ

Scientific Name (Nombre latino)
DIOSCOREA ALATA

Spanish Name (Nombre cubano)
ÑAME BLANCO

Yoruba Name (Nombre lucumí)
ICHÚ, OSÚRA

Scientific Name (Nombre latino)
DIOSCOREA PILOSIUSCULA

Spanish Name (Nombre cubano)
ÑAME VOLADOR,
ÑAME CIMARRÓN

Yoruba Name (Nombre lucumí)
ICHÚ

Scientific Name (Nombre latino)
EICHHORNIA AZUREA
(EICHHORNIA CRASSIPES, PONTEDERIA CRASSIPES)

Spanish Name (Nombre cubano)
FLOR DE AGUA

Yoruba Name (Nombre lucumí)
OLLUORO, OLLÓURO,
TANÁ FÚN FÚN, BODÓ

Scientific Name (Nombre latino)
ELAPHRIUM SIMARUBA
(BURSERA SIMARUBA)

Spanish Name (Nombre cubano)
ALMÁCIGO

Yoruba Name (Nombre lucumí)
IGGI ADDAMA, MOYÉ, ILÚKI

Scientific Name (Nombre latino)
ELEUSINE INDICA
(DACTYLOCTENIUM AEGYPTIUM)

Spanish Name (Nombre cubano)
PATA DE GALLINA

Yoruba Name (Nombre lucumí)
ERÁN, DEDÉ, ARÁOGU, OKLEPÚESU

Scientific Name (Nombre latino)
ERYTHRINA GLAUCA
(ERYTHRINA BERTEROANA)

Spanish Name (Nombre cubano)
PIÑON DE PITO

Yoruba Name (Nombre lucumí)
EFÉKE, YRIN

Scientific Name (Nombre latino)
EUPATORIUM ODORATUM (EUPATORIUM CANNABINUM)

Spanish Name (Nombre cubano)
ALBAHACA DE SABANA, TRAVESERA, ALBAHAQUILLA,
ROMPE ZARAGÜEY

Yoruba Name (Nombre lucumí)
TABATÉ, JAN

Scientific Name (Nombre latino)
EUPATORIUM VILLOSUM

Spanish Name (Nombre cubano)
ABRE CAMINO

Scientific Name (Nombre latino)
EUPHORBIA LACTEA
(EUPHORBIA PEPLUS)

Spanish Name (Nombre cubano)
CARDÓN

Yoruba Name (Nombre lucumí)
IKÁ, AGOGÓ

Scientific Name (Nombre latino)
EUPHORBIA PULCHERRIMA

Spanish Name (Nombre cubano)
FLOR DE PASCUA

Scientific Name (Nombre latino)
FICUS MEMBRANACEA

Spanish Name (Nombre cubano)
JAGÜEY

Yoruba Name (Nombre lucumí)
FIAPABBA, IGGI IGWÁ,
IGGI OKÉ, AFOMÁ, UENDO

Scientific Name (Nombre latino)
FICUS NITIDA

Spanish Name (Nombre cubano)
LAUREL DE INDIA

Yoruba Name (Nombre lucumí)
IGGINILE ITIRI, IGGI GAFIOFO

Scientific Name (Nombre latino)
FICUS RELIGIOSA

Spanish Name (Nombre cubano)
ÁLAMO

Yoruba Name (Nombre lucumí)
OFÁ, IGOLE, ABAILA, LLESO,
IGGOLE IKIYENYO, OFÁ

Scientific Name (Nombre latino)
GOSSYPIUM BARBADENSE

Spanish Name (Nombre cubano)
ALGODÓN

Yoruba Name (Nombre lucumí)
ORI ORO, EU, OÚ, OWÚ, KEOLI

Scientific Name (Nombre latino)
GOUANIA POLYGAMA

Spanish Name (Nombre cubano)
BEJUCO LEÑATERO,
BEJUCO DE CUBA

Yoruba Name (Nombre lucumí)
IDALLA

Scientific Name (Nombre latino)
GUAJUMA ULMIFOLIA
(GUAZUMA GUAZUMA)

Spanish Name (Nombre cubano)
GUÁSIMA

Yoruba Name (Nombre lucumí)
IGGI BONI

Scientific Name (Nombre latino)
HELIOTROPIUM INDICUM (HELIOTROPIUM
CAMPECHIANUM)

Spanish Name (Nombre cubano)
ALACRANCILLO

Yoruba Name (Nombre lucumí)
AGUÉYI

Scientific Name (Nombre latino)
HIBISCUS ABELMOSCHUS (ABELMOSCHUS ESCULENTUS)

Spanish Name (Nombre cubano)
AMBARINA

Yoruba Name (Nombre lucumí)
IYEYÉ-TANAEKO

Scientific Name (Nombre latino)
HIBISCUS ESCULENTUS

Spanish Name (Nombre cubano)
QUIMBOMBÓ

Yoruba Name (Nombre lucumí)
LILÁ, ALILÁ, ILÁ, ALLÁ

Scientific Name (Nombre latino)
HIBISCUS ROSA-SINENSIS

Spanish Name (Nombre cubano)
HIBISCU o MAR PACIFICO

Yoruba Name (Nombre lucumí)
EWE ATÒRI

Scientific Name (Nombre latino)
ILEX AQUIFOLIUM (ILEX MONTANA)

Spanish Name (Nombre cubano)
ACEBO DE SIERRA, ACEBO DE TIERRA

Yoruba Name (Nombre lucumí)
SUCUÍ

Scientific Name (Nombre latino)
INDIGOFERA TINCTORIA

Spanish Name (Nombre cubano)
AÑIL, INDIGO

Yoruba Name (Nombre lucumí)
YINIYA, ÑI

Scientific Name (Nombre latino)
IPOMOEA BATATAS

Spanish Name (Nombre cubano)
BONIATO

Yoruba Name (Nombre lucumí)
UNDUKÚMDUKÚ, KUÁNDUKU, ODUKÓ, CUCÚNDU
CUENDÚEN, CUCUNDUCÚ, CUCUDUCÚ

Scientific Name (Nombre latino)
IPOMOEA TUBEROSA

Spanish Name (Nombre cubano)
BEJUCO DE INDIO

Yoruba Name (Nombre lucumí)
CHINYO

Scientific Name (Nombre latino)
JAMBOS JAMBOS
(EUGENIA JAMBOS, EUGENIA CARYIOPHILLATA, JAMBOSA
CARYOPHYLLUS, CARYOPHYLLUS AROMATICUS)

Spanish Name (Nombre cubano)
POMARROSA

Yoruba Name (Nombre lucumí)
YILEBO, ECHICACHO

Scientific Name(Nombre latino)
JATROPHA DIVERSIFOLIA

Spanish Name (Nombre cubano)
PEREGRINA

Yoruba Name (Nombre lucumí)
ERO

Scientific Name (Nombre latino)
KALANCHOE PINNATA (BRY PINNATUM PINNATUM)

Spanish Name (Nombre cubano)
SIEMPRE VIVA, PRODIGIOSA, BELLADONA

Yoruba Name (Nombre lucumi)
EWE DUNDUN, EWE ODUNDUN

Scientific Name (Nombre latino)
LACTUCA SATIVA
(LACTUCA SCARIOLA)

Spanish Name (Nombre cubano)
LECHUGA

Yoruba Name (Nombre lucumí)
ILENKE, OGGÙ YÉYÉ

Scientific Name (Nombre latino)
LAGERSTROEMIA INDICA

Spanish Name (Nombre cubano)
ASTRONOMIA

Yoruba Name (Nombre lucumí)
TAKÉ

Scientific Name (Nombre latino)
LAVANDULA ANGUSTIFOLIA

Spanish Name (Nombre cubano)
LAVANDA

Scientific Name (Nombre latino)
LEPIDIUM VIRGINICUM

Spanish Name (Nombre cubano)
MASTUERZO, SABE LECCIÓN

Yoruba Name (Nombre lucumí)
ERIBO, ICHINI-CHINI, ERIBOSA, TÁN

Scientific Name (Nombre latino)
LEUCAENA GLAUCA

Spanish Name (Nombre cubano)
AROMA BLANCA

Yoruba Name (Nombre lucumi)
RIANI

Scientific Name (Nombre latino)
LONCHOCARPUS LATIFOLIUS

Spanish Name (Nombre cubano)
GUAMÁ DE COSTA

Yoruba Name (Nombre lucumí)
YERÉKETE, ADERE ODO

Scientific Name (Nombre latino)
LYCOPERSICUM ESCULENTUM

Spanish Name (Nombre cubano)
TOMATE

Yoruba Name (Nombre lucumí) |
CHOMA, ICAN, IGARE, YKAIE

Scientific Name (Nombre latino)
MANGIFERA INDICA

Spanish Name (Nombre cubano)
MANGO

Yoruba Name (Nombre lucumí)
AIRO, ORO, ELÉSO, ORUN BÉKE
ORO AYIMBO, OLOMBO

Scientific Name (Nombre latino)
MANIHOT ESCULENTA

Spanish Name (Nombre cubano)
YUCA

Yoruba Name (Nombre lucumí)
KOKOMADOCO, IBAGGUDDÁN, BAGGUDÁN

Scientific Name (Nombre latino)
MELIA AZEDERACH

Spanish Name (Nombre cubano)
PARAÍSO

Yoruba Name (Nombre lucumí)
IBAYO, YIYA

Scientific Name (Nombre latino)
MELOTHRIA GUADALUPENSIS

Spanish Name (Nombre cubano)
MELONCILLO

Scientific Name (Nombre latino)
MIMOSA PUDICA

Spanish Name (Nombre cubano)
SENSITIVA, VERGONZOSA, DORMIDERA

Yoruba Name (Nombre lucumí)
ERAN KUMI, ERAN LOYÓ,
OMIMI, YARANIMÓ

Scientific Name (Nombre latino)
MIRABILIS JALAPA

Spanish Name (Nombre cubano)
MARAVILLA

Yoruba Name (Nombre lucumí)
EWÉ ÒGUMO, EWÉ TANAPOSHO

Scientific Name (Nombre latino)
MOMORDICA CHARANTIA L

Spanish Name (Nombre cubano)
CUNDE AMOR,
AMOR SECO, ROMERILLO

Yoruba Name (Nombre lucumi)
ABERE OLOKO, ABARE, OJU AGUTAN

Scientific Name (Nombre latino)
MORINGA OLEIFERA

Spanish Name (Nombre cubano)
ACACIA, PARAISO

Scientific Name (Nombre latino)
MUSA PARADISIACA

Spanish Name (Nombre cubano)
PLATANO

Yoruba Name (Nombre lucumí)
OGGUEDE, OGUE GUERE

Scientific Name (Nombre latino)
NASTURTIUM OFFICINALE

Spanish Name (Nombre cubano)
BERRO

Yoruba Name (Nombre lucumí)
IGUÉRE, YEYÉ PEREGÚN

Scientific Name (Nombre latino)
NICOTIANA TABACUM, Var. HAVANENSIS

Spanish Name (Nombre cubano)
TABACO

Yoruba Name (Nombre lucumí)
ETÁBA, ACHÁ

Scientific Name (Nombre latino)
NYMPHAEA LOTUS

Spanish Name (Nombre cubano)
LIRIO DE AGUA, FLOR DE LOTO

Yoruba Name (Nombre lucumi)
ASHIBATA

Scientific Name (Nombre latino)
OCIMUM BASILICUM, Var. ANISATUM

Spanish Name (Nombre cubano)
ALBAHACA ANISADA

Yoruba Name (Nombre lucumí)
TONÓMIYO, ORORÓ, NISÉ

Scientific Name (Nombre latino)
OCIMUM BASILICUM, VAR. PURPUREUM

Spanish Name (Nombre cubano)
ALBAHACA MORADA

Yoruba Name (Nombre lucumí)
ORORÓ, FINI ADACHÉ

Scientific Name (Nombre latino)
OCIMUM MICRANTHUM

Spanish Name (Nombre cubano)
ALBAHACA DE CLAVO

Yoruba Name (Nombre lucumí)
BERENRÉ, ORORÓ

111

Scientific Name (Nombre latino)
OCIMUM SANCTUM
(CLINOPODIUM VULGARE)

Spanish Name (Nombre cubano)
ALBAHACA CIMARRONA

Yoruba Name (Nombre lucumí)
ORORÓ

Scientific Name (Nombre latino)
OREODOXA REGIA
(ROYSTONEA REGIA)

Spanish Name (Nombre cubano)
PALMA REAL

Yoruba Name (Nombre lucumi)
ILE CHANGO ORISSA, IGGI OPPWE OPE, ALABI CEFIDIYE,
ELUWERE, OLUWEKON

Scientific Name (Nombre latino)
ORIZA SATIVA

Spanish Name (Nombre cubano)
ARROZ

Yoruba Name (Nombre lucumí)
EUO, SINCOFA, IRÁSI, CHEQUEFA

Scientific Name (Nombre latino)
OXANDRA LANCEOLATA

Spanish Name (Nombre cubano)
YAYA

Yoruba Name (Nombre lucumí)
YAYA, ECHI

Scientific Name (Nombre latino)
PARALABATIA DICTYONEURA

Spanish Name (Nombre cubano)
CUCUYO

Yoruba Name (Nombre lucumí)
OFUNTANA

Scientific Name (Nombre latino)
PARITI TILIACEUM

Spanish Name (Nombre cubano)
MAJAGUA

Yoruba Name (Nombre lucumí)
MERENGUENE

117

Scientific Name (Nombre latino)
PARTHENIUM HYSTEROPHORUS

Spanish Name (Nombre cubano)
ARTEMISILLA

Yoruba Name (Nombre lucumí)
EWE IRII

118

Scientific Name (Nombre latino)
PASPALUM NOTATUM

Spanish Name (Nombre cubano)
HIERBA FINA

Yoruba Name (Nombre lucumi)
EWÉ GBEGÍ

Scientific Name (Nombre latino)
PELARGONIUM ODARATISSIMUM

Spanish Name (Nombre cubano)
GERANIO

Yoruba Name (Nombre lucumí)
PUPAYO

Scientific Name (Nombre latino)
PENNYWORT

Spanish Name (Nombre cubano)
PARAGUITA

Yoruba Name (Nombre lucumi)
EWÉ AKÒKO

Scientific Name (Nombre latino)
PERSEA GRATISSIMA

Spanish Name (Nombre cubano)
AGUACATE

Yoruba Name (Nombre lucumi)
ITOBI, OKUTARA ITÓBI, ODOFRE, BIMA, ACATARA

Scientific Name (Nombre latino)
PETIVERIA ALLIACEA

Spanish Name (Nombre cubano)
ANAMÚ

Yoruba Name (Nombre lucumí)
YENA, ANAMÚ, OCHISÁN

Scientific Name (Nombre latino)
PETROSELINUM CRISPUM

Spanish Name (Nombre cubano)
PEREJIL

Yoruba Name (Nombre lucumí)
ISAKO, IYADEDÉ

Scientific Name (Nombre latino)
PHYLLANTUS ACIDUS
(CICCA DISTICHA)

Yoruba Name (Nombre lucumí)
MEYELE ESO, AKIVARÉ

125

Scientific Name (Nombre latino)
PHYLLANTUS NIRURI

Spanish Name (Nombre cubano)
HIERBA DE LA NIÑA

Yoruba Name (Nombre lucumí)
NENE, NANI, ÑANI, NENÉ

Scientific Name (Nombre Latino)
PILEA MICROPHYLLA, L.

Spanish Name (Nombre cubano)
FRESCURA

Yoruba Name (Nombre lucumí)
KUYEKUYE, EDUN, EWE TUTU

Scientific Name (Nombre latino)
PINUS TROPICALIS
(PINUS CARIBAEA)

Spanish Name (Nombre cubano)
PINO

Yoruba Name (Nombre lucumí)OKILÓN, ORUKOÑIKÁN,
YEMAO

Scientific Name (Nombre latino)
PIPER ADUNCUM

Spanish Name (Nombre cubano)
PLATANILLO DE CUBA

Yoruba Name (Nombre lucumí)
OLÚBBO

Scientific Name (Nombre latino)
PIPER PELTATUM L.

Spanish Name (Nombre cubano)
CAISIMÓN

Yoruba Name (Nombre lucumi)
EWÉ BENERÍ, EWÉ ÒTÓ

Scientific Name (Nombre latino)
PISONIA ACULEATA

Spanish Name (Nombre cubano)
ZARZA

Yoruba Name (Nombre lucumí)
EGÚN, IGGI EGÚN, TIYÁ

Scientific Name (Nombre latino)
PISTIA STRATIOTES

Spanish Name (Nombre cubano)
LECHUGUILLA

Yoruba Name (Nombre lucumi)
OJU ORO

Scientific Name (Nombre latino)
PITHECELLOBIUM ARBOREUM

Spanish Name (Nombre cubano)
MORURO

Yoruba Name (Nombre lucumí)
ORUDAN, EFENKOKO

Scientific Name (Nombre latino)
PLANTAGO

Spanish Name (Nombre cubano)
LLANTEN O YANTEN

Scientific Name (Nombre latino)
PLUMBAGO SCADENS
(CORDIA GLOBOSA)

Spanish Name (Nombre cubano)
LEGAÑA, LAGAÑA DE AURA

Yoruba Name (Nombre lucumí)
IWAGO, ICOLEKOKÉ

Scientific Name (Nombre latino)
POEPPIGIA PROCERA

Spanish Name (Nombre cubano)
TÉNGUE, PALO TÉNGUE

Yoruba Name (Nombre lucumí)
ADEBESÚ, SONGA, LABAL, LABARÍ

Scientific Name (Nombre latino)
POINCIANA PULCHERRIMA

Spanish Name (Nombre cubano)
GUACAMAYA AMARILLA

Yoruba Name (Nombre lucumí)
ORUMAYA, PUPURUSA

137

Scientific Name (Nombre latino)
POINCIANA PULCHERRIMA

Spanish Name (Nombre cubano)
GUACAMAYA COLORADA

Yoruba Name (Nombre lucumí)
ORUMAYA, EWE PON,
KAMARERÉ, ERUNTOKO

Scientific Name (Nombre latino)
PORTULACA OLERACEA

Spanish Name (Nombre cubano)
VERDOLAGA

Yoruba Name (Nombre lucumí)
EKISÁN, PAPASÁN

Scientific Name (Nombre latino)
PROSOPIS CHILENSIS

Spanish Name (Nombre cubano)
ALGARROBO

Yoruba Name (Nombre lucumí)
EWE BÁNA

Scientific Name (Nombre latino)
PRUNUS OCCIDENTALIS

Spanish Name (Nombre cubano)
CUAJANI

Yoruba Name (Nombre lucumí)
MADDETÉO

Scientific Name (Nombre latino)
PSIDIUM GUAYAVA

Spanish Name (Nombre cubano)
GUAYABA

Yoruba Name (Nombre lucumí)
KENKU

Scientific Name (Nombre latino)
PUNICA GRANATUM

Spanish Name (Nombre cubano)
GRANADA

Yoruba Name (Nombre lucumí)
OROCO, MAYAKU, YAYEKU,
KANSORE, CHIMINÍ CHIMINÍ, AGBÁ

149

Scientific Name (Nombre latino)
RHIZOPHORA MANGLE
(AVICENNA NITIDA, RHIZOPHORA CANDEL)

Spanish Name (Nombre cubano)
MANGLE

Yoruba Name (Nombre lucumí)
EWE ATÍODO, KASIORO

Scientific Name (Nombre latino)
RHOEO DISCOLOR
(RHOEO SPATHACEA, TRADESCANTIA DISCOLOR)

Spanish Name (Nombre cubano)
CORDOBÁN, CORDOVÁN

Yoruba Name (Nombre lucumí)
PEREGÚN TUPÁ, PEREGÚN PUPPUÁ, PERUGÚN, TUPÁ,
DIELA, YERE GUN

Scientific Name (Nombre latino)
RICINUS COMMUNIS

Spanish Name (Nombre cubano)
TARTAGO, HIGUERETA

Yoruba Name (Nombre lucumí)
EWÉ ÒMÒ

146

Scientific Name (Nombre latino)
ROSA GALLICA

Spanish Name (Nombre cubano)
ROSA FRANCESA

Yoruba Name (Nombre lucumí)
TETELÍ, DIDEKERÉ

Scientific Name (Nombre latino)
ROSMARINUS OFFICINALIS

Spanish Name (Nombre cubano)
ROMERO

Yoruba Name (Nombre lucumí)
RE, PAGWABIMÁ

Scientific Name (Nombre latino)
ROUREA GLABRA

Spanish Name (Nombre cubano)
MATANEGRO

Yoruba Name (Nombre lucumí)
KONRI, KUKENKÉLEYO

Scientific Name (Nombre latino)
RUTA CHALEPENSIS

Spanish Name (Nombre cubano)
RUDA

Yoruba Name (Nombre lucumí)
ATOPÁ KUN

Scientific Name (Nombre latino)
SACCHARUM OFFICINARUM

Spanish Name (Nombre cubano)
CAÑA DE AZÚCAR

Yoruba Name (Nombre lucumí)
IGGUERÉ, IREKE, OREKÉ, EREKÉ

Scientific Name (Nombre latino)
SAGITTARIA INTERMEDIA

Spanish Name (Nombre cubano)
MALANGUILLA, SÁCU-SÁCU

Yoruba Name (Nombre lucumí)
KÓHO,

Scientific Name (Nombre latino)
SALVIA OFFICINALIS
(SALVIA SCLAREA)

Spanish Name (Nombre cubano)
SALVIA DE CASTILLA

Yoruba Name (Nombre lucumí)
KIRIWI

Scientific Name (Nombre latino)
SAPONARIA OFFICINALIS
(GOUANIA LUPULOIDES, GOUANIA POLYGAMA)

Spanish Name (Nombre cubano)
JABONCILLO

Yoruba Name (Nombre lucumí)
OBUENO, KEKERIONGO

Scientific Name (Nombre latino)
SAVIA SESSILLIFLORA

Spanish Name (Nombre cubano)
ARETILLO

Yoruba Name (Nombre lucumí)
GUANKÉ

Scientific Name (Nombre latino)
SCHAEFFERIA FRUTESCENS

Spanish Name (Nombre cubano)
AMANSA GUAPO

Yoruba Name (Nombre lucumí)
KUNINO

Scientific Name (Nombre latino)
SERJANIA LUPULINA
(SERJANIA DIVERSIFOLIA)

Spanish Name (Nombre cubano)
BEJUCO COLORADO

Yoruba Name (Nombre lucumí)
OBOLÓ

Scientific Name (Nombre latino)
SERJANIA PANICULATA

Spanish Name (Nombre cubano)
BEJUCO DE CORRALES

Yoruba Name (Nombre lucumí)
WÁNIRI

158

Scientific Name (Nombre latino)
SESAMUM INDICUM

Spanish Name (Nombre cubano)
AJONJOLÍ

Yoruba Name (Nombre lucumí)
AMATI

Scientific Name (Nombre latino)
SIDA CORDATA

Spanish Name (Nombre cubano)
BOTÓN DE ORO

Yoruba Name (Nombre lucumi)
EWE FIN, EWE OFIN

Scientific Name (Nombre latino)
SIMARUBA GLAUCA

Spanish Name (Nombre cubano)
PALO BLANCO

Yoruba Name (Nombre lucumi)
IGGI FUN

Scientific Name (Nombre latino)
SOLANUM HAVANENSE

Spanish Name (Nombre cubano)
AJÍ DE CHINA

Yoruba Name (Nombre lucumí)
ATÁ GUARÚ, ATÁ FINLANDI

162

Scientific Name (Nombre latino)
SOLANUM NIGRUM
(SOLANUM AMERICANUM, SOLANUM MODIFLURUM)

Spanish Name (Nombre cubano)
HIERBA MORA

Yoruba Name (Nombre lucumí)
ATORE, ATORÍ, EFODA,
EPODÚ, EGUNMO

Scientific Name (Nombre latino)
SPIGELIA ANTHELMIA

Spanish Name (Nombre cubano)
ESPIGELIS

Yoruba Name (Nombre lucumí)
MINIRÉ

Scientific Name (Nombre latino)
SWIETENIA MAHOGONY

Spanish Name (Nombre cubano)
CAOBA

Yoruba Name (Nombre lucumí)
AYÁN, ROCO

Scientific Name (Nombre latino)
TERMINALIA CATAPPA
(TERMINALIA GLAUCESCENS, TERMINALIA IVORENSIS)

Spanish Name (Nombre cubano)
ALMENDRO

Yoruba Name (Nombre lucumí)
ABUSÍ, IGGI, URE, ECUCI

Scientific Name (Nombre latino)
TERMINALIA INTERMEDIA

Spanish Name (Nombre cubano)
CHICHARRÓN DE MONTE

Yoruba Name (Nombre lucumí)
YENKÉ

167

Scientific Name (Nombre latino)
TOURNEFORTIA GNAPHALODES

Spanish Name (Nombre cubano)
INCIENSO DE PLAYA

Yoruba Name (Nombre lucumí)
EGBADDÓ

Scientific Name (Nombre latino)
TRIBULUS MAXIMUS

Spanish Name (Nombre cubano)
ABROJO

Yoruba Name (Nombre lucumí)
EGBELEGÚN, IGGILEGÚN

Scientific Name (Nombre latino)
TRIBULUS MAXIMUS
(KALSTROEMIA MAXIMA)

Spanish Name (Nombre cubano)
ABROJO TERRESTRE

Yoruba Name (Nombre lucumí)
CHORO, IGBELEGGÚN

Scientific Name (Nombre latino)
TRICHILIA HAVANENSIS

Spanish Name (Nombre cubano)
SIGUARAYA, CIGUARAYA

Yoruba Name (Nombre lucumí)
ATORI

Scientific Name (Nombre latino)
TRICHILIA HIRTA

Spanish Name (Nombre cubano)
CABO DE HACHA

Yoruba Name (Nombre lucumí)
ERÉ, IGGI NIKÁ, AKUDÍYICA

172

Scientific Name (Nombre latino)
VERBENA OFFICINALIS

Spanish Name (Nombre cubano)
VERBENA

Yoruba Name (Nombre lucumi)
EWÉ OGÁNGÁN

Scientific Name (Nombre latino)
VIGNA UNGUICULATA
(DOLICHOS SINENSIS, DOLICHOS LABLAB)

Spanish Name (Nombre cubano)
FRIJOL DE CARITA

Yoruba Name (Nombre lucumí)
ERE-É PIPÁ, ERECHÉ

Scientific Name (Nombre latino)
VITEX DONIANA

Spanish Name (Nombre cubano)
OFON, OFUN

Yoruba Name (Nombre lucumí)
MEREMIYÉ

175

Scientific Name (Nombre latino)
VITIS TILLIFOLIA

Spanish Name (Nombre cubano)
BEJUCO JÍMAGUA,
PARRA CIMARRONA

Yoruba Name (Nombre lucumí)
LOPAMÓ, AJARÁ MELLI

Scientific Name (Nombre latino)
XANTHOSOMA SAGITTIFOLIUM (XANTHOSOMA
VIOLACEUM, COLOCASIA ATIQUORUM)

Spanish Name (Nombre cubano)
MALANGA

Yoruba Name (Nombre lucumí)
IKOKU, ICHU, CHICÁ, COCO,
LLESCO, MARABABO

Scientific Name (Nombre latino)
ZANTHOXYLUM MARTINICENSE

Spanish Name (Nombre cubano)
AYÚA

Yoruba Name (Nombre lucumí)
ELEGÚN, IGGI ORO

Scientific Name (Nombre latino)
ZEA MAIS

Spanish Name (Nombre cubano)
MAIZ

Yoruba Name (Nombre Jucumi)
AGUADÓ, AGUADDÓ,
AGGUADÓ, ABADDO, AWADO, OKÁ

179

Scientific Name (Nombre latino)
ZEBRINA PURPUSII
(ZEBRINA PENDULA, TRADESCANZIA TRICOLOR)

Spanish Name (Nombre cubano)
CUCARACHA (ZEBRINA PENDULA), CUCARACHA MORADA
(ZEBRINA PURPUSII)

Yoruba Name (Nombre lucumí)
AÑAÍ

Spanish Name – Scientific Name Glossary (Glossario de Nombre cubano - Nombre latino)

ABRE CAMINO - EUPATORIUM VILLOSUM
ABROJO TERRESTRE - TRIBULUS MAXIMUS (KALSTROEMIA MAXIMA)
ABROJO -TRIBULUS MAXIMUS
ACACIA - MORINGA OLEIFERA
ACEBO DE SIERRA - ILEX AQUIFOLIUM (ILEX MONTANA)
ACEBO DE TIERRA - ILEX AQUIFOLIUM (ILEX MONTANA)
AGUACATE - PERSEA GRATISSIMA
AJÍ GUAGUAO - CAPSICUM BACCATUM
AJÍ DE CHINA - SOLANUM HAVANENSE
AJO - ALLIUM SATIVUM
AJONJOLÍ - SESAMUM INDICUM
ALACRANCILLO - HELIOTROPIUM INDICUM (HELIOTROPIUM CAMPECHIANUM)
ÁLAMO - FICUS RELIGIOSA
ALBAHACA ANISADA - OCIMUM BASILICUM, Var. ANISATUM
ALBAHACA DE CLAVO - OCIMUM MICRANTHUM
ALBAHACA DE SABANA - EUPATORIUM ODORATUM (EUPATORIUM CANNABINUM)
ALBAHACA CIMARRONA - OCIMUM SANCTUM (CLINOPODIUM VULGARE)
ALBAHACA MORADA - OCIMUM BASILICUM, VAR. PURPUREUM
ALBAHAQUILLA - EUPATORIUM ODORATUM (EUPATORIUM CANNABINUM)
ALGARROBO - PROSOPIS CHILENSIS
ALGODÓN - GOSSYPIUM BARBADENSE
ALMÁCIGO - ELAPHRIUM SIMARUBA (BURSERA SIMARUBA)
ALMENDRO - TERMINALIA CATAPPA (TERMINALIA GLAUCESCENS, TERMINALIA IVORENSIS)
ALTAMISA - AMBROSIA ARTEMISIFOLIA (COCHLEARIA CORONOPUS)
AMANSA GUAPO - SCHAEFFERIA FRUTESCENS
AMBARINA - HIBISCUS ABELMOSCHUS (ABELMOSCHUS ESCULENTUS)
AMOR SECO - MOMORDICA CHARANTIA L
ANAMÚ - PETIVERIA ALLIACEA
AÑIL - INDIGOFERA TINCTORIA
APASOTE - CHENOPODIUM AMBROSIODES

ARETILLO - SAVIA SESSILLIFLORA
AROMA BLANCA - LEUCAENA GLAUCA
ARROZ - ORIZA SATIVA
ARTEMISA - AMBROSIA ARTEMISIFOLIA (COCHLEARIA CORONOPUS)
ARTEMISILLA - PARTHENIUM HYSTEROPHORUS
ASTRONOMIA - LAGERSTROEMIA INDICA
ATEJE COMUN - CORDIA COLLOCOCCA
ATIPONLA - BOERHAAVIA ERECTA CARIBAEA
AYÚA - ZANTHOXYLUM MARTINICENSE
BEJUCO COLORADO - SERJANIA LUPULINA (SERJANIA DIVERSIFOLIA)
BEJUCO DE CORRALES - SERJANIA PANICULATA
BEJUCO DE CUBA - GOUANIA POLYGAMA
BEJUCO DE INDIO - IPOMOEA TUBEROSA
BEJUCO JÍMAGUA - VITIS TILLIFOLIA
BEJUCO LEÑATERO - GOUANIA POLYGAMA
BEJUCO UBÍ - CISSUS SICYOIDES (CISSUS QUADRANGULARIS)
BEJUCO UVÍ - CISSUS SICYOIDES (CISSUS QUADRANGULARIS)
BELLADONA - KALANCHOE PINNATA (BRYOPHYLLUM PINNATUM)
BERRO - NASTURTIUM OFFICINALE
BIJA - BIXA ORELLANA
BLEDO - AMARANTHUS VIRIDIS
BONIATO - IPOMOEA BATATAS
BOTÓN DE ORO - SIDA CORDATA
CABO DE HACHA - TRICHILIA HIRTA
CAFÉ - COFFEA ARABICA
CAIMITO - CHRYSOPHILLUM CAINITO
CAISIMÓN - PIPER PELTATUM L.
CALABAZA - CUCURBITA MAXIMA
CALALÚ - CALALU
CAMPANA - DATURA SUAVEOLENS
CAÑA BRAVA - BAMBUSA VULGARIS
CAÑA DE AZÚCAR - SACCHARUM OFFICINARUM

CANELA DE MONTE - CINNAMOMUM CASSIA (CINNAMOMUM ZEYLANICUM)

CANELA DE CHINA - CINNAMOMUM CASSIA (CINNAMOMUM ZEYLANICUM)

CANUTILLO - COMMELINA ELEGANS

CAOBA - SWIETENIA MAHOGONY

CARDÓN - EUPHORBIA LACTEA (EUPHORBIA PEPLUS)

CEDRO - CEDRELA MEXICANA (CITRUS MEDICA)

CEIBA - CEIBA PENTANDRA (CEIBA CASEARIA)

CIGUARAYA - TRICHILIA HAVANENSIS

COCO - COCOS NUCIFERA

CRESTA DE GALLO - CELOSIA ARGENTEA

CARDO SANTO - ARGEMONE MEXICANA

CEBOLLA - ALLIUM CEPA

CHAMICO - DATURA STRAMONIUM

CHICHARRÓN DE MONTE - TERMINALIA INTERMEDIA

COJATE, COATE, COLONIA - ALPINIA AROMATICA (ALPINIA SPECIOSA SCHUM)

CORDOBÁN - RHOEO DISCOLOR (RHOEO SPATHACEA, TRADESCANTIA DISCOLOR)

CORDOVÁN - RHOEO DISCOLOR (RHOEO SPATHACEA, TRADESCANTIA DISCOLOR)

COROJO - ACROCOMIA CRISPA (ELAEIS GUINEENSIS)

CUABA - AMYRIS BALSAMIFERA

CUAJANI - PRUNUS OCCIDENTALIS

CUCARACHA (ZEBRINA PENDULA) - ZEBRINA PURPUSII (ZEBRINA PENDULA, TRADESCANZIA TRICOLOR)

CUCARACHA MORADA (ZEBRINA PURPUSII) - ZEBRINA PURPUSII (ZEBRINA PENDULA, TRADESCANZIA TRICOLOR)

CUCUYO - PARALABATIA DICTYONEURA

CULANTRILLO DE POZO - ADIANTUM TENERUM (ADIANTUM CAPILLUS VENERIS)

CUNDE AMOR - MOMORDICA CHARANTIA L

DÁGAME - CALYCOPHILLUM CANDIDISSIMUM

DEJAME SENTARME - CISSAMPELOS MUCRONATA

DORMIDERA - MIMOSA PUDICA

ESCLABIOSA - CAPRARIA BIFLORA

ESCLAVIOSA - CAPRARIA BIFLORA

ESPIGELIS - SPIGELIA ANTHELMIA

FRIJOL DE CARITA - VIGNA UNGUICULATA (DOLICHOS SINENSIS, DOLICHOS LABLAB)

FLOR DE AGUA - EICHHORNIA AZUREA (EICHHORNIA CRASSIPES, PONTEDERIA CRASSIPES)

FLOR DE LOTO - NYMPHAEA LOTUS

FLOR DE PASCUA -EUPHORBIA PULCHERRIMA

FRAILECILLO, CAIRECILLO DE MONTE - ADENOROPIUM GOSSYPIFOLIUM

FRESCURA - PILEA MICROPHYLLA, L.

FRUTA BOMBA - CARICA PAPAYA

GALÁN DE DÍA - CESTRUM DIURNUM

GERANIO - PELARGONIUM ODARATISSIMUM

GRAMA - CYNODON DACTYLON (AGROPYRUM REPENS)

GRANADA - PUNICA GRANATUM

GUACAMAYA AMARILLA - POINCIANA PULCHERRIMA

GUACAMAYA COLORADA - POINCIANA PULCHERRIMA

GUAMÁ DE COSTA - LONCHOCARPUS LATIFOLIUS

GUANÁBANA - ANNONA MURICATA

GUANINA - CASSIA OCCIDENTALIS (CASSIA TORA)

GUARA - CUPANIA CUBENSIS

GUÁSIMA - GUAJUMA ULMIFOLIA (GUAZUMA GUAZUMA)

GUAYABA - PSIDIUM GUAYAVA

GUENGUERÉ - CORCHORUS OLITORIUS

GÜIRA - CRESCENTIA CUJETE

HIBISCU/MAR PACIFICO - HIBISCUS ROSA-SINENSIS

HIERBA DE LA NIÑA - PHYLLANTUS NIRURI

HIERBA FINA -PASPALUM NOTATUM

HIERBA HEDIONDA - CASSIA OCCIDENTALIS (CASSIA TORA)

HIERBA MORA - SOLANUM NIGRUM (SOLANUM AMERICANUM, SOLANUM MODIFLURUM)

HIGUERETA - RICINUS COMMUNIS

INCIENSO - ARTEMISIA ABROTANUM (ARTEMISIA CAMPHORATA)

INCIENSO DE PLAYA - TOURNEFORTIA GNAPHALODES

INDIGO - INDIGOFERA TINCTORIA

JABONCILLO - SAPONARIA OFFICINALIS (GOUANIA LUPULOIDES, GOUANIA POLYGAMA)

JAGÜEY - FICUS MEMBRANACEA

LAGAÑA DE AURA - PLUMBAGO SCADENS (CORDIA GLOBOSA)
LAUREL DE INDIA - FICUS NITIDA
LAVANDA - LAVANDULA ANGUSTIFOLIA
LECHUGA - LACTUCA SATIVA (LACTUCA SCARIOLA)
LECHUGUILLA - PISTIA STRATIOTES
LEGAÑA - PLUMBAGO SCADENS (CORDIA GLOBOSA)
LIMÓN - CITRUS LIMON
LIRIO DE AGUA - NYMPHAEA LOTUS
LLANTEN/ YANTEN - PLANTAGO
MABOA - CAMERARIA LATIFOLIA
MAIZ - ZEA MAIS
MAJAGUA - PARITI TILIACEUM
MALANGA - XANTHOSOMA SAGITTIFOLIUM (XANTHOSOMA VIOLACEUM, COLOCASIA ATIQUORUM)
MALANGUILLA - SAGITTARIA INTERMEDIA
MALVA TÈ - CORCHORUS OLITORIUS
MAMEY COLORADO - ACHRAS ZAPOTA
MANGLE - RHIZOPHORA MANGLE (AVICENNA NITIDA, RHIZOPHORA CANDEL)
MANGO - MANGIFERA INDICA
MANÍ - ARACHIS HYPOGAEA
MAR PACIFICO/HIBISCU - HIBISCUS ROSA-SINENSIS
MARAVILLA - MIRABILIS JALAPA
MASTUERZO- LEPIDIUM VIRGINICUM
MATANEGRO - ROUREA GLABRA
MELÓN DE AGUA - CITRULLUS CITRULLUS (CITRULLUS LANATUS)
MELONCILLO - MELOTHRIA GUADALUPENSIS
MORURO - PITHECELLOBIUM ARBOREUM
ÑAME BLANCO - DIOSCOREA ALATA
ÑAME CIMARRÓN - DIOSCOREA PILOSIUSCULA
ÑAME VOLADOR - DIOSCOREA PILOSIUSCULA
NARANJA - CITRUS AURANTIUM (CITRUS SINENSIS)
NARANJA AGRIA - CITRUS AURANTIUM, VAR. AMARA (CITRUS VULGARIS)
PALMA REAL - OREODOXA REGIA (ROYSTONEA REGIA)

PALO BLANCO - SIMARUBA GLAUCA
PALO CAFÉ - AMAIOUA CORYMBOSA
PALO CAJA - ALLOPHYLLUS COMINIA
PALO TENGUE - POEPPIGIA PROCERA
PAPAYA - CARICA PAPAYA
PARAÍSO - MELIA AZEDERACH
PARRA CIMARRONA - VITIS TILLIFOLIA
PATA DE GALLINA - CYNODON DACTYLON (AGROPYRUM REPENS)
PATA DE GALLINA - ELEUSINE INDICA (DACTYLOCTENIUM AEGYPTIUM)
PARAISO - MORINGA OLEIFERA
PARAGUITA - PENNYWORT
PLATANO - MUSA PARADISIACA
PEONÍA - ABRUS PRECATORIUS
PEREGRINA - JATROPHA DIVERSIFOLIA
PEREJIL - PETROSELINUM CRISPUM
PIMIENTA DE GUINEA - AFRAMOMUN MELEGUETA
PIÑA BLANCA - ANANAS ANANAS (ANANAS COMOSUS)
PINO -PINUS TROPICALIS (PINUS CARIBAEA)
PIÑON BOTIJA - CURCAS CURCAS (JATROPHA CURCAS)
PIÑON DE PITO - ERYTHRINA GLAUCA (ERYTHRINA BERTEROANA)
PLATANILLO DE CUBA - PIPER ADUNCUM
POMARROSA - JAMBOS JAMBOS (EUGENIA JAMBOS, EUGENIA CARYIOPHILLATA, JAMBOSA
    CARYOPHYLLUS, CARYOPHYLLUS AROMATICUS)
PRODIGIOSA - KALANCHOE PINNATA (BRYOPHYLLUM PINNATUM)
ROMERILLO - MOMORDICA CHARANTIA L
ROMERO - ROSMARINUS OFFICINALIS
ROSA FRANCESA - ROSA GALLICA
RUDA - RUTA CHALEPENSIS
QUIMBOMBÓ - HIBISCUS ESCULENTUS
QUITA MALDICIÓN - CAESALPINIA BONDUC
RASPA LENGUA - CASEARIA HIRSUTA
ROMPE ZARAGÜEY - EUPATORIUM ODORATUM (EUPATORIUM CANNABINUM)

SABE LECCIÓN - LEPIDIUM VIRGINICUM
SÁCU-SÁCU - SAGITTARIA INTERMEDIA
SALVIA DE CASTILLA - SALVIA OFFICINALIS (SALVIA SCLAREA)
SENSITIVA - MIMOSA PUDICA
SIEMPRE VIVA - KALANCHOE PINNATA (BRYOPHYLLUM PINNATUM)
SIGUARAYA - TRICHILIA HAVANENSIS
TÉ DEL DIABLO - DATURA STRAMONIUM
TABACO - NICOTIANA TABACUM, Var. HAVANENSIS
TARTAGO - RICINUS COMMUNIS
TÉNGUE - POEPPIGIA PROCERA
TOMATE - LYCOPERSICUM ESCULENTUM
TRAVESERA - EUPATORIUM ODORATUM (EUPATORIUM CANNABINUM)
VERBENA - VERBENA OFFICINALIS
VERDOLAGA - PORTULACA OLERACEA
VERGONZOSA - MIMOSA PUDICA
VICARIA - CATHARANTHUS ROSEUS
YAGRUMA - CECROPIA PELTATA
YAYA - OXANDRA LANCEOLATA
YANTEN/LLANTEN -PLANTAGO
YEDRA - ANREDERA SPICATA (HEDERA HELIX)
YUCA - MANIHOT ESCULENTA
ZAPOTE - ACHRAS SAPOTE
ZARZA - PISONIA ACULEATA

Yoruba Name - Scientific Name Glossary (Glossario de Nombre lucumí - Nombre latino)

ABÁDDO - ZEA MAIS
ABAILA - FICUS RELIGIOSA
ABARE - MOMORDICA CHARANTIA L
ABERE OLOKO - MOMORDICA CHARANTIA L
ABERIKUNLÓ - CAESALPINIA BONDUC
ABUSÍ - TERMINALIA CATAPPA (TERMINALIA GLAUCESCENS, TERMINALIA IVORENSIS)
ACATARA - PERSEA GRATISSIMA
ACHÁ - NICOTIANA TABACUM, Var. HAVANENSIS
ADEBESÚ- POEPPIGIA PROCERA
ADERE ODO - LONCHOCARPUS LATIFOLIUS
ADDÓ - CURCAS CURCAS (JATROPHA CURCAS)
AFOMÁ- FICUS MEMBRANACEA
AGAGWÁN - CUPANIA CUBENSIS
AGBÁ - PUNICA GRANATUM
AGBÉ- CRESCENTIA CUJETE
AGBÉYE - CITRULLUS CITRULLUS (CITRULLUS LANATUS)
AGGOGÓ - DATURA SUAVEOLENS
AGGUADÓ - ZEA MAIS
AGGÜÉ- CRESCENTIA CUJETE
AGOGÓ - ARGEMONE MEXICANA
AGOGÓ - DATURA SUAVEOLENS
AGOGÓ - EUPHORBIA LACTEA (EUPHORBIA PEPLUS)
AGUADÓ - ZEA MAIS
AGUADDÓ - ZEA MAIS
AGUE TUTÚ - CITRULLUS CITRULLUS (CITRULLUS LANATUS)
AGUÉYI - HELIOTROPIUM INDICUM (HELIOTROPIUM CAMPECHIANUM)
AIRO - MANGIFERA INDICA
AJARÁ MELLI - VITIS TILLIFOLIA
AKIVARÉ - PHYLLANTUS ACIDUS (CICCA DISTICHA)
AKUDÍYICA - TRICHILIA HIRTA

AKUNU - CURCAS CURCAS (JATROPHA CURCAS)
ALABA - CEIBA PENTANDRA (CEIBA CASEARIA)
ALABI - OREODOXA REGIA (ROYSTONEA REGIA)
ALILÁ - HIBISCUS ESCULENTUS
ALLÁ - HIBISCUS ESCULENTUS
ALLÉCOFOLE - CHRYSOPHILLUM CAINITO
ALU DESO GUERE - ALLIUM SATIVUM
ALÚBOSA - ALLIUM CEPA
ALUMOFÓ - CURCAS CURCAS (JATROPHA CURCAS)
AMATI - SESAMUM INDICUM
ANAMÚ - PETIVERIA ALLIACEA
AÑAÍ - ZEBRINA PURPUSII (ZEBRINA PENDULA, TRADESCANZIA TRICOLOR)
APÓ - AMAIOUA CORYMBOSA
ARABBÁ - CEIBA PENTANDRA (CEIBA CASEARIA)
ARÁGGUO - CEIBA PENTANDRA (CEIBA CASEARIA)
ARÁOGU- ELEUSINE INDICA (DACTYLOCTENIUM AEGYPTIUM)
ASABÁ (IGGI ARABBÁ) - CEIBA PENTANDRA (CEIBA CASEARIA)
ASÁN - CHRYSOPHILLUM CAINITO
ASHIBATA - NYMPHAEA LOTUS
ATÁ - AFRAMOMUN MELEGUETA
ATÁ - CAPSICUM BACCATUM
ATÁ FINLANDI - SOLANUM HAVANENSE
ATÁ GUARÚ - SOLANUM HAVANENSE
ATARE - AFRAMOMUN MELEGUETA
ATIPONLA - BOERHAAVIA ERECTA CARIBAEA
ATOPÁ KUN - RUTA CHALEPENSIS
ATORE - SOLANUM NIGRUM (SOLANUM AMERICANUM, SOLANUM MODIFLURUM)
ATORÍ - SOLANUM NIGRUM (SOLANUM AMERICANUM, SOLANUM MODIFLURUM)
ATORI - TRICHILIA HAVANENSIS
AWADO - ZEA MAIS
AYÁN - SWIETENIA MAHOGONY
AYÉCO FOLÉ - CHRYSOPHILLUM CAINITO

AYEGUÉ - CASSIA OCCIDENTALIS (CASSIA TORA)
BAGGUDÁN - MANIHOT ESCULENTA
BASIGÜE - ADENOROPIUM GOSSYPIFOLIUM
BERENRÉ - OCIMUM MICRANTHUM
BIMA - PERSEA GRATISSIMA
BODÓ - EICHHORNIA AZUREA (EICHHORNIA CRASSIPES, PONTEDERIA CRASSIPES)
BUSIA - ARACHIS HYPOGAEA
CALALÚ - CALALU
CARODI COTONÉMBO - COMMELINA ELEGANS
CARRODDO - COMMELINA ELEGANS
CEFIDIYÉ - OREODOXA REGIA (ROYSTONEA REGIA)
CHEQUEFA - ORIZA SATIVA
CHICÁ - XANTHOSOMA SAGITTIFOLIUM (XANTHOSOMA VIOLACEUM, COLOCASIA ATIQUORUM)
CHIMINÍ CHIMINÍ - PUNICA GRANATUM
CHINYO - IPOMOEA TUBEROSA
CHORO - TRIBULUS MAXIMUS (KALSTROEMIA MAXIMA)
COCO - XANTHOSOMA SAGITTIFOLIUM (XANTHOSOMA VIOLACEUM, COLOCASIA ATIQUORUM)
COTOLO - COMMELINA ELEGANS
COTONEMBO - CYNODON DACTYLON (AGROPYRUM REPENS)
COTONEMBO - COMMELINA ELEGANS
CUCUDUCÚ - IPOMOEA BATATAS
CUCÚNDU CUENDÚEN - IPOMOEA BATATAS
CUCUNDUCÚ - IPOMOEA BATATAS
DEDÉ - CINNAMOMUM CASSIA (CINNAMOMUM ZEYLANICUM)
DEDÉ - CORCHORUS SILIQUOSUS
DEDÉ - ELEUSINE INDICA (DACTYLOCTENIUM AEGYPTIUM)
DENGO - CYNODON DACTYLON (AGROPYRUM REPENS)
DIDEKERÉ - ROSA GALLICA
DIDONA - ALPINIA AROMATICA (ALPINIA SPECIOSA SCHUM)
DIELA - RHOEO DISCOLOR (RHOEO SPATHACEA, TRADESCANTIA DISCOLOR)
ECHI - OXANDRA LANCEOLATA

ECHICACHO - JAMBOS JAMBOS (EUGENIA JAMBOS, EUGENIA CARYIOPHILLATA,
JAMBOSA CARYOPHYLLUS, CARYOPHYLLUS AROMATICUS)
ECUCI - TERMINALIA CATAPPA (TERMINALIA GLAUCESCENS, TERMINALIA IVORENSIS)
EDUN - PILEA MICROPHYLLA, L.
EEKANNA EKUN - ARGEMONE MEXICANA
EFENKOKO - PITHECELLOBIUM ARBOREUM
EFÁ - ARACHIS HYPOGAEA
EFÉKE - ERYTHRINA GLAUCA (ERYTHRINA BERTEROANA)
EFO - CORCHORUS OLITORIUS
EFODA - SOLANUM NIGRUM (SOLANUM AMERICANUM, SOLANUM MODIFLURUM)
EGBADDÓ - TOURNEFORTIA GNAPHALODES
EGBOIBO - ANANAS ANANAS (ANANAS COMOSUS)
EGUNMO - SOLANUM NIGRUM (SOLANUM AMERICANUM, SOLANUM MODIFLURUM)
EGBELEGÚN - TRIBULUS MAXIMUS
EGGUÉLE KERI - CISSUS SICYOIDES (CISSUS QUADRANGULARIS)
EGGWÁ- CRESCENTIA CUJETE
EGUN - PISONIA ACULEATA
EGWÁ - CRESCENTIA CUJETE
EKÁNCHACHAETÉ - COFFEA ARABICA
EKISÁN - PORTULACA OLERACEA
EKPÓ - ACROCOMIA CRISPA (ELAEIS GUINEENSIS)
ELEGGUÉ - CYNODON DACTYLON (AGROPYRUM REPENS)
ELEGUEDDÉ - CUCURBITA MAXIMA
ELEGÚN - ZANTHOXYLUM MARTINICENSE
ELÉSO - MANGIFERA INDICA
ELLA SRO - ALLIUM CEPA
ELUÉCO - CEIBA PENTANDRA (CEIBA CASEARIA)
ELUWERE - OREODOXA REGIA (ROYSTONEA REGIA)
ELÚWERE - CEIBA PENTANDRA (CEIBA CASEARIA)
EMÍ - ACHRAS ZAPOTA
EPÁ - ARACHIS HYPOGAEA
EPAMILBO - ARACHIS HYPOGAEA

EPÓ - ACROCOMIA CRISPA (ELAEIS GUINEENSIS)
EPO PUPO - ACROCOMIA CRISPA (ELAEIS GUINEENSIS)
EPODÚ - SOLANUM NIGRUM (SOLANUM AMERICANUM, SOLANUM MODIFLURUM)
ERAN - CYNODON DACTYLON (AGROPYRUM REPENS)
ERÁN- ELEUSINE INDICA (DACTYLOCTENIUM AEGYPTIUM)
ERAN KUMI - MIMOSA PUDICA
ERAN LOYÓ - MIMOSA PUDICA
ERÉ - TRICHILIA HIRTA
ERE-É PIPÁ, ERECHÉ - VIGNA UNGUICULATA (DOLICHOS SINENSIS, DOLICHOS LABLAB)
EREKÉ - SACCHARUM OFFICINARUM
ERIBO - LEPIDIUM VIRGINICUM
ERIBOSA - LEPIDIUM VIRGINICUM
ERO - JATROPHA DIVERSIFOLIA
ERUNTOKO - POINCIANA PULCHERRIMA
ESÁ- CITRUS AURANTIUM (CITRUS SINENSIS)
ESO - PHYLLANTUS ACIDUS (CICCA DISTICHA)
ETÁBA - NICOTIANA TABACUM, Var. HAVANENSIS
EU - GOSSYPIUM BARBADENSE
EUO - ORIZA SATIVA
EWA - ARACHIS HYPOGAEA
EWÉ ABAMODA - KALANCHOE PINNATA (BRYOPHYLLUM PINNATUM)
EWÉ AKÒKO - PENNYWORT
EWE ATÍODO - RHIZOPHORA MANGLE (AVICENNA NITIDA, RHIZOPHORA CANDEL)
EWE ATÒRI - HIBISCUS ROSA-SINENSIS
EWE AYO - CAESALPINIA BONDUC
EWE BÁNA - PROSOPIS CHILENSIS
EWÉ BENERÍ - PIPER PELTATUM L.
EWÉ DUNDUN - KALANCHOE PINNATA (BRYOPHYLLUM PINNATUM)
EWE ECHÉNLA - DATURA STRAMONIUM
EWE ELÉNU - CASEARIA HIRSUTA
EWE FIN - SIDA CORDATA
EWÉ GBEGÍ - PASPALUM NOTATUM

EWE IRII - PARTHENIUM HYSTEROPHORUS
EWÉ ODUNDUN - KALANCHOE PINNATA (BRYOPHYLLUM PINNATUM)
EWE OFIN - SIDA CORDATA
EWE OFÓ - DATURA STRAMONIUM
EWÉ OGÁNGÁN - VERBENA OFFICINALIS
EWÉ ÒGUMO - MIRABILIS JALAPA
EWÉ ÒMÒ - RICINUS COMMUNIS
EWÉ ÒTÓ - PIPER PELTATUM L.
EWE PON - POINCIANA PULCHERRIMA
EWÉ TANAPOSHO - MIRABILIS JALAPA
EWE TELE - AMARANTHUS CAUDATUS
EWE TETÉ (CHAURÉ KUE KUE E WEIKO) - AMARANTHUS VIRIDIS
EWE TOMODE - CASSIA OCCIDENTALIS (CASSIA TORA)
EWE TUTU - PILEA MICROPHYLLA, L.
EWERENJENJÉ - ABRUS PRECATORIUS
FIAPABBA - FICUS MEMBRANACEA
FINI ADACHÉ - OCIMUM BASILICUM, VAR. PURPUREUM
GAÚTI - CAPRARIA BIFLORA
GUAGUAO - CAPSICUM BACCATUM
GUANKÉ - SAVIA SESSILLIFLORA
GUARÁ - CUPANIA CUBENSIS
GWÁNILLO - ANNONA MURICATA
IBAGGUDDÁN - MANIHOT ESCULENTA
IBAKUÁ MINOCUÍ - COMMELINA ELEGANS
IBAYO - MELIA AZEDERACH
IBEKUÉ - CARICA PAPAYA
IBÉPPE - CARICA PAPAYA
ICHOMA - LYCOPERSICUM ESCULENTUM
ICAN - LYCOPERSICUM ESCULENTUM
ICAN - LYCOPERSICUM ESCULENTUM
ICARE - LYCOPERSICUM ESCULENTUM
ICHINI-CHINI - LEPIDIUM VIRGINICUM

ICHOMA - LYCOPERSICUM ESCULENTUM

ICHU - XANTHOSOMA SAGITTIFOLIUM (XANTHOSOMA VIOLACEUM, COLOCASIA ATIQUORUM)

ICHÚ - DIOSCOREA ALATA

ICHÚ - DIOSCOREA PILOSIUSCULA

ICOLEKOKÉ - PLUMBAGO SCADENS (CORDIA GLOBOSA)

IDALLA - GOUANIA POLYGAMA

IDEFÉ - CARICA PAPAYA

IGBÁ - CRESCENTIA CUJETE

IGBEELEGÚN - ARGEMONE MEXICANA

IGBELEGGÚN - TRIBULUS MAXIMUS (KALSTROEMIA MAXIMA)

IGGI - CECROPIA PELTATA

IGGI - TERMINALIA CATAPPA (TERMINALIA GLAUCESCENS, TERMINALIA IVORENSIS)

IGGI ADDAMA - ELAPHRIUM SIMARUBA (BURSERA SIMARUBA)

IGGI BIRÉ - ALLOPHYLLUS COMINIA

IGGI BONI - GUAJUMA ULMIFOLIA (GUAZUMA GUAZUMA)

IGGI EGÚN - PISONIA ACULEATA

IGGI EPÓ KAN - CINNAMOMUM CASSIA (CINNAMOMUM ZEYLANICUM)

IGGI FÚN - SIMARUBA GLAUCA

IGGI GAFIOFO - FICUS NITIDA

IGGI IGWÁ- FICUS MEMBRANACEA

IGGI KAN - COFFEA ARABICA

IGGI NIKÁ - TRICHILIA HIRTA

IGGI OKÉ - FICUS MEMBRANACEA

IGGI OLORUN - CEIBA PENTANDRA (CEIBA CASEARIA)

IGGI OMÓ FUNFÚN - ANNONA MURICATA

IGGI OPPWÉ - OREODOXA REGIA (ROYSTONEA REGIA)

IGGI ORO - ZANTHOXYLUM MARTINICENSE

IGGIFERE - AMAIOUA CORYMBOSA

IGGILEGÚN - TRIBULUS MAXIMUS

IGGINILE ITIRI - FICUS NITIDA

IGGOLÉ - FICUS RELIGIOSA

IGOLE - FICUS RELIGIOSA

IGGUERÉ - SACCHARUM OFFICINARUM
IGUÉRE - NASTURTIUM OFFICINALE
IKÁ - ARGEMONE MEXICANA
IKÁ - EUPHORBIA LACTEA (EUPHORBIA PEPLUS)
IKOKU - XANTHOSOMA SAGITTIFOLIUM (XANTHOSOMA VIOLACEUM, COLOCASIA ATIQUORUM)
IKIYÉNYO - FICUS RELIGIOSA
ILÁ - HIBISCUS ESCULENTUS
ILÉ CHANGÓ ORISSÁ - OREODOXA REGIA (ROYSTONEA REGIA)
ILENKE - LACTUCA SATIVA (LACTUCA SCARIOLA)
ILÚKI - ELAPHRIUM SIMARUBA (BURSERA SIMARUBA)
IRÁSI - ORIZA SATIVA
IREKE - SACCHARUM OFFICINARUM
IROKO - CEIBA PENTANDRA (CEIBA CASEARIA)
IROKO TERÉ - CEIBA PENTANDRA (CEIBA CASEARIA)
IROKO-AWO - CEIBA PENTANDRA (CEIBA CASEARIA)
ISAKO - PETROSELINUM CRISPUM
ITAKO - ANREDERA SPICATA (HEDERA HELIX)
ITAKÚN - CITRULLUS CITRULLUS (CITRULLUS LANATUS)
ITOBI - PERSEA GRATISSIMA
IWAGO - PLUMBAGO SCADENS (CORDIA GLOBOSA)
IYADEDÉ - PETROSELINUM CRISPUM
IYERÁN - CYNODON DACTYLON (AGROPYRUM REPENS)
IYEYÉ-TANAEKO - HIBISCUS ABELMOSCHUS (ABELMOSCHUS ESCULENTUS)
JAN - EUPATORIUM ODORATUM (EUPATORIUM CANNABINUM)
JARA–JARA - CASSIA OCCIDENTALIS (CASSIA TORA)
JASISAN KROPOMU - CASSIA OCCIDENTALIS (CASSIA TORA)
JOKOIO EWÉCO - ALLIUM SATIVUM
KAMARERÉ - POINCIANA PULCHERRIMA
KANSORE - PUNICA GRANATUM
KARODO - COMMELINA ELEGANS
KASIORO - RHIZOPHORA MANGLE (AVICENNA NITIDA, RHIZOPHORA CANDEL)
KEKERIONGO - SAPONARIA OFFICINALIS (GOUANIA LUPULOIDES, GOUANIA POLYGAMA)

KENKU - PSIDIUM GUAYAVA
KEOLI - GOSSYPIUM BARBADENSE
KIRIWI - SALVIA OFFICINALIS (SALVIA SCLAREA)
KÓHO - SAGITTARIA INTERMEDIA
KOKOMADOCO - MANIHOT ESCULENTA
KONRI - ROUREA GLABRA
KORODO - COMMELINA ELEGANS
KOROKOLO - CINNAMOMUM CASSIA (CINNAMOMUM ZEYLANICUM)
KOROSÁN - CITRUS AURANTIUM, VAR. AMARA (CITRUS VULGARIS)
KOTONIO, OFI, NECENTÉN - ADIANTUM TENERUM (ADIANTUM CAPILLUS VENERIS)
KUÁNDUKU - IPOMOEA BATATAS
KUKENKÉLEYO - ROUREA GLABRA
KUNINO - SCHAEFFERIA FRUTESCENS
KUYEKUYE - PILEA MICROPHYLLA, L.
LABAL - POEPPIGIA PROCERA
LABARÍ - POEPPIGIA PROCERA
LACHEO - CORDIA COLLOCOCCA
LÁNGWE - CORDIA COLLOCOCCA
LARA - CECROPIA PELTATA
LARO - CECROPIA PELTATA
LÉCHU IBAYÉ - CAMERARIA LATIFOLIA
LIBBE KUKO - CELOSIA ARGENTEA
LILÁ - HIBISCUS ESCULENTUS
LINIDDI - AMBROSIA ARTEMISIFOLIA (COCHLEARIA CORONOPUS)
LIONSE - CALYCOPHILLUM CANDIDISSIMUM
LLESCO - XANTHOSOMA SAGITTIFOLIUM (XANTHOSOMA VIOLACEUM, COLOCASIA ATIQUORUM)
LLESO - FICUS RELIGIOSA
LOASO - AMYRIS BALSAMIFERA
LOBÉ - AMARANTHUS VIRIDIS
LOPAMÓ - VITIS TILLIFOLIA
LORO - CECROPIA PELTATA
LUFI - ACROCOMIA CRISPA (ELAEIS GUINEENSIS)

MADDETÉO - PRUNUS OCCIDENTALIS
MARABABO - XANTHOSOMA SAGITTIFOLIUM (XANTHOSOMA VIOLACEUM, COLOCASIA ATIQUORUM)
MAYAKU- PUNICA GRANATUM
MERÉMBE - ALLOPHYLLUS COMINIA
MEREMIYÉ - VITEX DONIANA
MERENGUENE - PARITI TILIACEUM
MEYELÉ - PHYLLANTUS ACIDUS (CICCA DISTICHA)
MINI - COMMELINA ELEGANS
MINIRÉ - SPIGELIA ANTHELMIA
MINSELO - ARTEMISIA ABROTANUM (ARTEMISIA CAMPHORATA)
MOYÉ - ELAPHRIUM SIMARUBA (BURSERA SIMARUBA)
NANI - PHYLLANTUS NIRURI
ÑANI - PHYLLANTUS NIRURI
NENE - PHYLLANTUS NIRURI
ÑENÉ - PHYLLANTUS NIRURI
NICHULARAFÚN - ANNONA MURICATA
NISÉ - OCIMUM BASILICUM, Var. ANISATUM
ÑI - INDIGOFERA TINCTORIA
OBI - COCOS NUCIFERA
OBIMOTIGWÁ - COFFEA ARABICA
OBOLÓ - SERJANIA LUPULINA (SERJANIA DIVERSIFOLIA)
OBUENO - SAPONARIA OFFICINALIS (GOUANIA LUPULOIDES, GOUANIA POLYGAMA)
OBURO - ALPINIA AROMATICA (ALPINIA SPECIOSA SCHUM)
OBBURUKÚ - CITRUS AURANTIUM (CITRUS SINENSIS)
OBBURUKÚ - CITRUS AURANTIUM (CITRUS SINENSIS)
OCHISÁN - PETIVERIA ALLIACEA
ODOFRE - PERSEA GRATISSIMA
ODUKÓ - IPOMOEA BATATAS
OEN - BIXA ORELLANA
OFÁ - FICUS RELIGIOSA
OFUNTANA - PARALABATIA DICTYONEURA
OGGÚ - CECROPIA PELTATA

OGGÚ YÉYÉ - LACTUCA SATIVA (LACTUCA SCARIOLA)
OGGUEDÉ - MUSA PARADISIACA
OGGUGÚ - CECROPIA PELTATA
OGGURE - CITRULLUS CITRULLUS (CITRULLUS LANATUS)
OGÓE FUSÉ - CHRYSOPHILLUM CAINITO
OGUE GUERE - MUSA PARADISIACA
OGUGUN - CECROPIA PELTATA
OGÚN GUN - CECROPIA PELTATA
OÍN - ALLOPHYLLUS COMINIA
OJU AGUTAN - MOMORDICA CHARANTIA L
OJU ORO - PISTIA STRATIOTES
OKÁ - ZEA MAIS
OKILÓN - PINUS TROPICALIS (PINUS CARIBAEA)
OKLEPÚESU - ELEUSINE INDICA (DACTYLOCTENIUM AEGYPTIUM)
OKUTARA ITÓBI - PERSEA GRATISSIMA
OLÉ IYÉTEBE - CURCAS CURCAS (JATROPHA CURCAS)
OLINE - CHENOPODIUM AMBROSIODES
OLLÓURO - EICHHORNIA AZUREA (EICHHORNIA CRASSIPES, PONTEDERIA CRASSIPES)
OLLUORO - EICHHORNIA AZUREA (EICHHORNIA CRASSIPES, PONTEDERIA CRASSIPES)
OLOBOTUYA - CURCAS CURCAS (JATROPHA CURCAS)
OLÓMBO - CITRUS AURANTIUM (CITRUS SINENSIS)
OLÓMBO - CITRUS LIMON
OLÚBBO - PIPER ADUNCUM
OLUWEKÓN - OREODOXA REGIA (ROYSTONEA REGIA)
OMATIWAOSEGÜI- COFFEA ARABICA
OMÍ DUDU - COFFEA ARABICA
OMIMI - MIMOSA PUDICA
OPÉ - OREODOXA REGIA (ROYSTONEA REGIA)
OPEPÉ, ROKÓ - CEDRELA MEXICANA (CITRUS MEDICA)
OPPÓYIBO - ANANAS ANANAS (ANANAS COMOSUS)
OREKÉ - SACCHARUM OFFICINARUM
ORI ORO - GOSSYPIUM BARBADENSE

ORO - MANGIFERA INDICA
ORO AYIMBO - MANGIFERA INDICA
OROCO - PUNICA GRANATUM
ORÓCO - CITRUS LIMON
OROLOCUM- CITRUS AURANTIUM (CITRUS SINENSIS)
ORÓMBO - CITRUS AURANTIUM (CITRUS SINENSIS)
OROMBOUEUÉ - CITRUS LIMON
ORORÓ - OCIMUM MICRANTHUM
ORORÓ - OCIMUM BASILICUM, Var. ANISATUM
ORORÓ - OCIMUM SANCTUM (CLINOPODIUM VULGARE)
ORORÓ - OCIMUM BASILICUM, VAR. PURPUREUM
ORÚ - ALPINIA AROMATICA (ALPINIA SPECIOSA SCHUM)
ORUDAN - PITHECELLOBIUM ARBOREUM
ORUFIRÍN, TOÍRO - CESTRUM DIURNUM
ORUKOÑIKÁN - PINUS TROPICALIS (PINUS CARIBAEA)
ORUMAYA - POINCIANA PULCHERRIMA
ORUN BÉKE - MANGIFERA INDICA
OSAEYÍMBO - CITRUS AURANTIUM (CITRUS SINENSIS)
OSÁM - CHRYSOPHILLUM CAINITO
OSÁN - CITRUS AURANTIUM (CITRUS SINENSIS)
OSINA BONA - COFFEA ARABICA
OSÚRA - DIOSCOREA ALATA
OÚ - GOSSYPIUM BARBADENSE
OWÚ - GOSSYPIUM BARBADENSE
OYÉUN - CASSIA OCCIDENTALIS (CASSIA TORA)
OYEUSÁ - CASSIA OCCIDENTALIS (CASSIA TORA)
OYÉ - CITRULLUS CITRULLUS (CITRULLUS LANATUS)
PAGWABIMÁ - ROSMARINUS OFFICINALIS
PÁIME - ADENOROPIUM GOSSYPIFOLIUM
PAPASAN - PORTULACA OLERACEA
PERUGÚN - RHOEO DISCOLOR (RHOEO SPATHACEA, TRADESCANTIA DISCOLOR)
PEREGÚN PUPPUÁ - RHOEO DISCOLOR (RHOEO SPATHACEA, TRADESCANTIA DISCOLOR)

PEREGÚN TUPÁ - RHOEO DISCOLOR (RHOEO SPATHACEA, TRADESCANTIA DISCOLOR)
PUPAYO - PELARGONIUM ODARATISSIMUM
PUPURUSA - POINCIANA PULCHERRIMA
RE - ROSMARINUS OFFICINALIS
RIANI - LEUCAENA GLAUCA
ROCO - SWIETENIA MAHOGONY
SINCOFA - ORIZA SATIVA
SONGA - POEPPIGIA PROCERA
SUCUÍ - ILEX AQUIFOLIUM (ILEX MONTANA)
TABATÉ - EUPATORIUM ODORATUM (EUPATORIUM CANNABINUM)
TÁN - LEPIDIUM VIRGINICUM
TANÁ FÚN FÚN - EICHHORNIA AZUREA (EICHHORNIA CRASSIPES, PONTEDERIA CRASSIPES)
TAKÉ - LAGERSTROEMIA INDICA
TETELÍ - ROSA GALLICA
TIYÁ - PISONIA ACULEATA
TONÓMIYO - OCIMUM BASILICUM, Var. ANISATUM
TUMAYÁ - CYNODON DACTYLON (AGROPYRUM REPENS)
TUPÁ - RHOEO DISCOLOR (RHOEO SPATHACEA, TRADESCANTIA DISCOLOR)
TURARÉ - ARTEMISIA ABROTANUM (ARTEMISIA CAMPHORATA)
UENDO - FICUS MEMBRANACEA
UNDUKÚMDUKÚ - IPOMOEA BATATAS
URÉ - TERMINALIA CATAPPA (TERMINALIA GLAUCESCENS, TERMINALIA IVORENSIS)
WÁNIRI - SERJANIA PANICULATA
YAASO - CASSIA OCCIDENTALIS (CASSIA TORA)
YARANIMÓ - MIMOSA PUDICA
YAYA - OXANDRA LANCEOLATA
YAYEKU - PUNICA GRANATUM
YENA - PETIVERIA ALLIACEA
YENKÉ - TERMINALIA INTERMEDIA
YERE GUN- RHOEO DISCOLOR (RHOEO SPATHACEA, TRADESCANTIA DISCOLOR)
YERÉKETE - LONCHOCARPUS LATIFOLIUS

YERÉOBO - CASEARIA HIRSUTA
YEYÉ PEREGÚN - NASTURTIUM OFFICINALE
YILEBO - JAMBOS JAMBOS (EUGENIA JAMBOS, EUGENIA CARYIOPHILLATA, JAMBOSA CARYOPHYLLUS, CARYOPHYLLUS AROMATICUS)
YKAIE - LYCOPERSICUM ESCULENTUM
YIYA - MELIA AZEDERACH
YRIN - ERYTHRINA GLAUCA (ERYTHRINA BERTEROANA)
YRIN - ERYTHRINA GLAUCA (ERYTHRINA BERTEROANA)

CPSIA information can be obtained
at www.ICGtesting.com
Printed in the USA
LVHW081922200523
747569LV00007B/101